Cursor AI Simplified

A Beginner-Friendly Guide to Harnessing Artificial Intelligence's Coding Superpowers

Taylor S. Alverton

Table of Contents

Introduction

Cursor AI is a groundbreaking tool designed to bridge the gap between traditional coding and the emerging possibilities of artificial intelligence. It has transformed the way developers approach coding tasks, offering solutions that simplify, accelerate, and enhance the overall programming experience. Built on the familiar framework of Visual Studio Code, Cursor AI integrates seamlessly into existing workflows, providing a unique blend of accessibility and innovation. This tool empowers users by automating repetitive tasks, offering intelligent suggestions, and enabling real-time edits, all while maintaining the precision and control developers rely on.

The promise of Cursor AI lies in its ability to cater to a diverse audience. For beginners, it demystifies the complexities of coding, turning what could be an intimidating endeavor into an approachable and enjoyable journey. By automating many of the initial hurdles, such as project setup and boilerplate code generation, Cursor AI allows new developers to focus on learning and experimenting. For experienced developers, it acts as a powerful productivity booster, streamlining workflows and allowing them to dedicate more time to creative problem-solving and innovation. In essence, Cursor AI makes coding simpler, faster, and more efficient, opening doors to opportunities that were previously limited by time and effort constraints.

Despite its transformative potential, Cursor AI remains underexplored by many, particularly those just beginning their journey into AI-assisted development. This guide aims to address the gap in beginner-friendly resources, providing clear, step-by-step instructions and insights that simplify the learning curve. While many existing tutorials dive directly into advanced projects, this book takes a different approach. It starts at the very beginning, ensuring that readers understand not just how to use Cursor AI but also why it works the way it does. This foundational understanding enables users to not only follow along but to innovate and adapt the tool to their specific needs.

This guide is written with a broad audience in mind. It is tailored for beginners who may be exploring the world of AI-assisted coding for the first time, offering them a structured path to proficiency. It also serves as a valuable resource for intermediate developers seeking to boost their productivity by leveraging AI's capabilities. Even curious learners, who may not yet be developers but are intrigued by the intersection of artificial intelligence and coding, will find this book an engaging and practical introduction.

By the end of this guide, readers will have a comprehensive understanding of Cursor AI, from its core features to its advanced functionalities. More importantly, they will feel empowered to harness its capabilities, whether to build their first project or to redefine how they approach coding altogether. Cursor AI represents the future of development, and this book is your roadmap to mastering it.

Chapter 1: Getting Started with Cursor AI

Downloading and Installing Cursor AI

Cursor AI is designed to be both accessible and user-friendly, making the process of downloading and setting it up straightforward. Whether you're a complete beginner or an experienced developer, getting started with Cursor AI involves just a few essential steps. The following guide will walk you through the entire process, ensuring you're ready to unlock the potential of this powerful AI-driven tool.

To begin, navigate to the official Cursor AI website by searching "Cursor AI" on your preferred search engine or directly visiting the link provided in official documentation. The homepage prominently displays a "Download for Free" button, making it clear and convenient for users. Clicking this button initiates the download process, and the setup file, approximately 120 MB in size, will be downloaded to your device. Be sure to have a stable internet connection during this process, as interruptions could cause delays or errors in downloading the file.

Once the file has been downloaded, locate it in your system's designated download folder. Double-click the setup file to launch the installation wizard. The wizard will guide you step-by-step through the installation process. You'll be prompted to agree to the terms and conditions, select a destination folder for the installation, and confirm other basic settings. For most users, the default options are sufficient, but you can customize these settings if needed. After confirming your choices, click "Install" and wait for the process to complete.

System requirements are another key consideration to ensure smooth operation. Cursor AI is compatible with most modern operating systems, including Windows, macOS, and certain distributions of Linux. Your system should ideally have at least 4GB of RAM and a dual-core processor, although higher specifications will enhance performance, especially when working with larger codebases or running resource-intensive tasks. Make sure your device has sufficient storage space, not just for the installation but also for additional components or extensions you might add later.

Once installed, the application will prompt you to launch it. The first launch is an exciting moment, as you're introduced to Cursor AI's sleek interface, which is modeled closely on Visual Studio Code. If you've used VS Code before, you'll find the interface familiar and easy to navigate, which significantly reduces the learning curve.

Initial Configuration

After successfully installing Cursor AI, the next step is to configure it to suit your workflow and preferences. This initial setup is vital to ensure that the tool aligns with how you work, whether you're a beginner exploring the basics or an experienced developer diving into advanced projects. The configuration process includes importing extensions, adjusting privacy settings, and customizing preferences.

One of the first prompts you'll encounter is the option to import settings and extensions from Visual Studio Code. Since Cursor AI is built on the VS Code framework, it allows you to carry over your favorite extensions, key bindings, and workspace settings. This feature is particularly beneficial for developers who already have a well-established workflow in VS Code. To import these settings, simply select the "Import Extensions" option during the initial setup. Cursor AI will automatically detect and sync compatible extensions from your VS Code installation.

For those starting from scratch, Cursor AI offers a clean slate. You can explore the built-in tools and features without the influence of pre-configured settings. This is an excellent opportunity for beginners to learn Cursor AI in its purest form, free from potential distractions or complexities introduced by imported extensions.

Privacy settings are another critical aspect of the initial configuration. Cursor AI provides two primary options: standard mode and privacy mode. Standard mode allows the application to collect anonymized telemetry data to improve its services, while privacy mode restricts data collection entirely. Enabling privacy mode ensures that your code and prompts remain confidential, making it an ideal choice for developers working on sensitive projects. To enable privacy mode, navigate to the "Preferences" menu during setup and toggle the privacy mode option. It's worth noting that even in privacy mode, certain features may require minimal data sharing for functionality, but Cursor AI emphasizes transparency and user control in these cases.

Cursor AI also allows you to customize its interface and functionality to match your personal preferences. From the "Settings" menu, you can adjust themes, font sizes, and key bindings. For instance, if you prefer a dark mode interface for reduced eye strain during long coding sessions, Cursor AI provides several visually appealing options. You can also set up shortcuts for frequently used commands, streamlining your workflow and saving time.

By taking the time to complete these initial configurations, you'll create an environment that feels intuitive and comfortable. This step not only enhances your productivity but also ensures that you're getting the most out of Cursor AI's powerful features.

First Look at Cursor AI

When you launch Cursor AI for the first time, you're greeted with a sleek and intuitive interface that closely resembles Visual Studio Code. This design choice makes Cursor AI immediately familiar to developers who have used VS Code before while remaining accessible to beginners who are new to coding environments. The interface is thoughtfully organized, with key features and tools positioned for easy access.

The main window is divided into several sections. On the left, you'll find the file explorer, which displays the directory structure of your current project. This area allows you to quickly navigate between files and folders. The central pane is the editor, where you write and edit your code. The editor supports multiple tabs, enabling you to work on several files simultaneously. On the right, you'll notice the AI chat window, which can be activated with a simple shortcut. This is where Cursor AI truly shines, as it provides context-aware suggestions, code explanations, and interactive features to enhance your coding experience.

One of Cursor AI's standout features is its seamless integration into existing workflows. Whether you're starting a new project or working on an existing one, Cursor AI adapts to your needs. You can open a folder directly from the file menu, just as you would in Visual Studio Code, and Cursor AI will automatically index your codebase. This indexing process allows the AI to understand your project's structure, making its suggestions and edits more accurate and relevant.

The command palette is another powerful feature that enhances navigation and functionality. Activated with a simple shortcut, the command palette allows you to search for commands, open files, and access settings without leaving the keyboard. This feature is particularly useful for speeding up repetitive tasks and maintaining focus during development.

Cursor AI also supports a wide range of programming languages, frameworks, and extensions. From Python and JavaScript to React and Tailwind CSS, the editor is equipped to handle diverse coding needs. You can customize the language and framework settings to align with your project requirements, ensuring that Cursor AI provides the most relevant assistance.

For beginners, Cursor AI offers a gentle introduction to coding. The AI chat window can explain code snippets, suggest improvements, and even generate boilerplate code for new projects. This interactive support reduces the intimidation factor often associated with learning to code, making Cursor AI an invaluable tool for those just starting their journey.

In summary, the first look at Cursor AI reveals a tool that is both familiar and innovative. Its thoughtful design, robust features, and seamless integration into existing workflows make it a game-changer for developers of all skill levels. Whether you're exploring coding for the first time or seeking ways to optimize your workflow, Cursor AI provides a solid foundation to achieve your goals.

Chapter 2: Core Features of Cursor AI

AI Chat Window

The AI Chat Window in Cursor AI serves as a central hub for real-time interaction with the tool, bridging the gap between traditional coding practices and the power of artificial intelligence. This feature enables developers to seamlessly generate, modify, and understand code within the context of their projects, all through conversational prompts. Accessing the chat interface is straightforward: a single shortcut, `Ctrl` + `L` on Windows or `Command` + `L` on Mac, opens the chat window to the right of the editor. This simplicity makes it an integral part of the Cursor AI workflow, catering to both beginners and seasoned developers.

At its core, the chat interface is designed to handle a variety of tasks. Its context-aware functionality allows it to provide intelligent suggestions based on the active project. For example, a user working on a

React application can ask the chat to generate a new component, and it will do so in a manner consistent with the project's structure and coding standards. Beyond code generation, the chat is an invaluable resource for understanding and debugging existing code. Users can highlight a section of code, paste it into the chat, and ask for an explanation or suggestions for improvement.

Generating code is one of the chat window's most practical applications. For instance, a developer can prompt the AI with a request like, "Create a login form using HTML and CSS with a gradient background." The chat responds by generating the necessary code, which can be reviewed and applied directly into the project. This capability eliminates the need to manually write repetitive boilerplate code, allowing developers to focus on higher-level problem-solving and creativity.

Another significant use of the chat interface is making adjustments to existing code. For example, suppose a developer wants to change the styling of a navigation bar. By highlighting the relevant code and asking the AI to "Make the navigation bar responsive and add hover effects," the chat will provide updated code snippets tailored to the request. This interactive editing process reduces the time spent on trial-and-error coding and enhances productivity.

The chat interface also supports commands that integrate external resources. Users can link documentation, files, or even URLs for the AI to reference. For example, a developer working with a new JavaScript library can provide its official documentation link and ask the AI to implement specific features based on it. This capability expands the tool's utility, making it adaptable to a wide range of coding scenarios.

Inline Editing

Inline editing is a feature of Cursor AI that enables users to make targeted adjustments to their code directly within the editor. This approach is particularly useful for modifying specific sections without disrupting the overall project workflow. The functionality is accessed using the shortcut `Ctrl + K` on Windows or `Command + K` on Mac. Once activated, users can select a portion of code, provide instructions for the changes they want, and see the updates applied in real time.

One common application of inline editing is modifying visual elements. For instance, a developer working on a webpage might want to change the background color of a section. By selecting the relevant CSS code and using the inline editor, they can instruct the AI with a command like, "Change the background color to a gradient of blue and green." The updated code is generated instantly and displayed in a diff view, allowing the developer to review and apply the changes.

Another example is adding new components to an existing project. Suppose a developer is building an e-commerce site and needs a product card component. By highlighting a placeholder div and instructing the AI to "Create a product card component with an image, title, price, and add-to-cart button," the inline editor generates the required HTML and CSS. This targeted editing approach streamlines the process of incorporating new features, especially in complex projects.

Inline editing also excels at revising text content. For instance, a developer updating a website's footer can highlight the existing content and prompt the AI to "Update the footer text to include the company's new address and contact information." The revised text is provided in seconds, reducing the need for manual edits and ensuring consistency across the codebase.

The feature is further enhanced by its ability to generate and display diffs for every change. This ensures transparency, as developers can see exactly what modifications are being made before accepting them. Inline editing thus combines precision and efficiency, making it an essential tool for both small tweaks and substantial revisions.

Composer Tool

The Composer Tool is one of Cursor AI's most powerful features, designed for creating and managing multiple files or components simultaneously. It is particularly useful for developers working on large-scale projects where maintaining consistency and efficiency is critical. To access the Composer, users can enable it in the settings and then activate it using the shortcut `Ctrl + I` on Windows or `Command + I` on Mac.

Once the Composer is open, it provides a workspace for drafting and generating complex code structures. For instance, a developer building a website can use the Composer to create multiple pages, such as a home page, an about page, and a contact page, all in one session. By specifying the project framework and style preferences, such as Next.js and Tailwind CSS, the AI generates the necessary files with consistent formatting and design elements.

The Composer Tool's ability to understand project context is a game-changer. For example, when building a landing page for a consultant, a user can prompt the AI with, "Create a landing page with a navbar, social media links, and a contact form." The Composer not only generates the required HTML, CSS, and JavaScript files but also ensures that components like the navbar are reusable across different pages.

Another application of the Composer is in creating boilerplate code for web applications. For instance, a developer can instruct the AI to "Set up a React project with a Redux store and authentication flow." The Composer generates the necessary files, such as the Redux store configuration, authentication components, and routing setup, saving hours of manual work.

The Composer Tool also excels at making batch updates to a codebase. Suppose a developer wants to add a footer component to all pages of a website. By specifying this in the Composer, the AI identifies the relevant files and integrates the footer component seamlessly. This capability is especially valuable in collaborative projects, where maintaining uniformity across multiple contributors' work is crucial.

In summary, the Composer Tool transforms how developers approach large-scale coding tasks. By automating the creation and management of multiple components, it enhances productivity and ensures consistency. Whether building a web application or creating a complete project structure, the Composer Tool provides a robust and efficient solution.

Chapter 3: Advanced Features

Model Integration

Cursor AI provides a versatile environment that supports multiple AI models, enabling users to tailor the tool's performance based on their specific needs. Switching between these models is an intuitive process, designed to cater to developers working on diverse projects. Whether you're using Claude 3.5 for its nuanced understanding of natural language or OpenAI's GPT models for their broad coding capabilities, Cursor AI ensures seamless integration with these cutting-edge technologies.

To switch between models, users can navigate to the settings menu in Cursor AI, where all available models are listed. Selecting a model is as simple as clicking on its name. Each model offers unique strengths: some excel in conversational contexts, making them ideal for debugging and code explanation, while others are optimized for generating code or managing large-scale projects.

Cursor AI allows you to experiment with these options, encouraging you to identify the model that best suits your workflow.

Adding custom models via API keys is another powerful feature that extends Cursor AI's utility. Developers with access to proprietary or third-party AI models can integrate them into Cursor AI by entering the appropriate API key. For instance, if a user wishes to utilize a model from OpenAI's extensive suite, they can obtain an API key from their OpenAI account and input it into Cursor AI's settings. The tool verifies the key and integrates the model, making it accessible alongside the default options.

This ability to add custom models is particularly beneficial for organizations or individuals with specialized needs. For example, a company working on domain-specific applications might use a fine-tuned AI model trained on proprietary data. By integrating this model into Cursor AI, the team can leverage its expertise directly within their development workflow. The flexibility of switching between default and custom models allows developers to harness the strengths of multiple AIs, tailoring their environment for maximum productivity.

Codebase Indexing

One of Cursor AI's standout features is its ability to build embeddings of the codebase for better navigation and searchability. This indexing process enables the tool to understand the structure and context of a project, enhancing its ability to provide relevant suggestions and execute accurate edits.

When a folder is opened in Cursor AI, the tool automatically indexes the codebase by analyzing its files, directories, and the relationships between them. This indexing creates an internal map of the project, allowing the AI to navigate through the code efficiently. For developers, this means that Cursor AI can understand the context of a specific file or variable, making its interactions more precise and effective.

The search function in Cursor AI is a direct application of this indexing. It enables users to locate files, variables, or functions within large projects quickly. By pressing a simple shortcut, such as `Ctrl + P` or using the command palette, developers can enter a search query and receive instant results. For instance, searching for a function name like `calculateTotal` will bring up all instances of the function in the project, along with clickable links to navigate to its definition or usage.

This feature is invaluable in large-scale projects with complex codebases. For example, a developer working on a multi-module application can use the search function to trace how a particular variable is passed across different files. Instead of manually scouring the codebase, they can rely on Cursor AI's indexing to surface the relevant details in seconds.

The indexing also enhances Cursor AI's chat and inline editing capabilities. When a developer asks the chat to explain a specific section of code or make adjustments, the tool references the indexed map to provide context-aware responses. This ensures that suggestions align with the project's overall structure and style, minimizing errors and inconsistencies.

Image-to-Code Conversion

Cursor AI's image-to-code feature is a revolutionary tool that bridges the gap between design and development. By uploading an image, such as a mockup or design file from tools like Figma, developers can generate corresponding HTML and CSS code. This feature simplifies the process of translating visual designs into functional code, making it a game-changer for front-end development.

To use this feature, developers can drag and drop an image file into the Cursor AI interface or upload it through the command palette. Once the image is uploaded, they can provide specific instructions, such as "Create an HTML file that replicates this form" or "Generate a responsive layout based on this design." Cursor AI processes the image and generates the requested code, which can then be reviewed, edited, and integrated into the project.

The output often includes a combination of HTML elements and CSS styling, replicating the layout, colors, and typography of the design. For example, uploading an image of a login form might produce a structured HTML file with labeled input fields, buttons, and accompanying CSS for styling. Developers can further customize the code to suit their project's requirements.

Despite its advantages, the image-to-code feature has certain limitations. The accuracy of the generated code depends on the clarity and simplicity of the input image. Complex designs with intricate details may result in incomplete or inaccurate outputs. Additionally, while the tool excels at creating static layouts, dynamic functionality, such as form validation or interactive elements, must be implemented manually.

To achieve the best results, developers should follow a few best practices. First, ensure that the input image is clear and well-defined, with minimal visual noise. High-resolution images are preferred, as they provide more detail for the AI to analyze. Second, break down complex designs into smaller components and process them individually. This approach allows Cursor AI to focus on specific sections, improving the quality of the output. Finally, review and refine the generated code to align it with the project's coding standards and functional requirements.

The image-to-code feature not only accelerates the development process but also fosters collaboration between designers and developers. By reducing the time and effort required to translate designs into code, Cursor AI enables teams to focus on innovation and creativity. This feature exemplifies the tool's mission to simplify and enhance the coding experience, making it an indispensable asset for modern development workflows.

Chapter 4: Practical Applications

Building a project from scratch using Cursor AI is an intuitive and streamlined process, thanks to its AI-driven features and seamless integration with modern frameworks. By following a step-by-step approach, developers—whether beginners or experienced—can efficiently set up, structure, and enhance their projects. In this example, we'll create a React-based web application to demonstrate Cursor AI's capabilities in simplifying the development process.

The first step is to ensure Cursor AI is installed and configured. If you haven't already set it up, refer to the previous sections of this guide for detailed instructions on installation and initial configuration. Once Cursor AI is ready, open the application and start by creating a new folder for your project. It's best to name the folder something descriptive, such as "MyReactApp," to keep your work organized. This can be done through the Cursor AI interface or directly via your file explorer.

Next, access the terminal within Cursor AI by navigating to the terminal panel or using the integrated terminal feature. This terminal functions just like the one in Visual Studio Code, allowing you to execute commands to set up and manage your project. Begin by initializing a React application using the `npx create-react-app` command followed by the name of your project. For example:

bash

Copy code

```
npx create-react-app myreactapp
```

This command generates the boilerplate code for a React application, including essential files and folders such as `src`, `public`, and `node_modules`. Cursor AI's indexing feature will automatically recognize the new files and map the project structure, making it easier for the AI to provide context-aware suggestions.

Once the React application has been created, open the project folder in Cursor AI. You can do this by selecting "Open Folder" from the file menu or dragging and dropping the folder into the application. With the project now loaded, Cursor AI's AI-powered tools come into play.

Let's start by customizing the application. Navigate to the `src` folder and locate the `App.js` file. This file serves as the entry point for the React application and contains the main component. Highlight the boilerplate code within `App.js` and activate Cursor AI's inline editing feature using `Ctrl + K` or `Command + K`. Provide a clear instruction, such as "Replace this boilerplate with a landing page that includes a navigation bar, a welcome message, and a call-to-action button."

Within seconds, Cursor AI will generate the updated code. For instance, it might add a `<nav>`

element with links, a `<header>` section with a welcome message, and a `<button>` element for the call-to-action. The AI will also ensure that the styling matches a cohesive design. If needed, you can refine the output by providing additional instructions, such as "Make the navigation bar sticky" or "Style the button with a gradient background."

With the main component in place, you can now expand your application by adding new components. For example, let's create a "Features" section to highlight the application's functionality. Use the Composer tool (`Ctrl + I` or `Command + I`) to instruct Cursor AI: "Create a Features component with three feature cards. Each card should have an icon, a title, and a description." The Composer generates a new `Features.js` file and automatically imports it into `App.js`.

To enhance interactivity, you can integrate state management using React's `useState` hook. For instance, suppose you want the call-to-action button to toggle a modal. Highlight the button's code and use the chat interface (`Ctrl + L` or `Command + L`) to instruct Cursor AI: "Add a modal that opens when this button is clicked and closes when a close button inside the modal is clicked." The AI will generate the modal component and update the button's `onClick` handler to manage the modal state.

Styling the application is equally straightforward with Cursor AI. If you're using a CSS framework like Tailwind CSS, instruct the AI to "Install Tailwind CSS and configure it for this project." Cursor AI will guide you through the installation steps, including adding the necessary dependencies and updating configuration files. Once Tailwind is set up, you can use it to style components by providing class names directly in the JSX or instructing Cursor AI to apply specific styles.

Finally, test the application by running it locally. Use the terminal to execute the following command:

bash

Copy code

```
npm start
```

This launches the development server and opens the application in your default web browser at http://localhost:3000. Review the application's functionality and design, making adjustments as needed using Cursor AI's tools.

The process of building a React-based web application with Cursor AI demonstrates its ability to simplify and accelerate development. By leveraging its AI-powered features for code generation, component creation, and styling, you can focus on creating a functional and visually appealing application without getting bogged down by repetitive tasks or boilerplate setup. Whether you're building a personal project, a portfolio site, or a prototype, Cursor AI empowers you to bring your ideas to life efficiently and effectively.

Real-Time Edits and Iterations

Real-time edits and iterations are where Cursor AI truly shines, allowing developers to modify project components seamlessly with the Inline Editor. This feature is designed to enhance efficiency by enabling precise, context-aware edits without disrupting the overall workflow. Whether it's adding functionality, refining aesthetics, or adjusting layouts, Cursor AI's Inline Editor simplifies the process while maintaining a fluid development experience.

To use the Inline Editor, you begin by selecting the portion of code you wish to modify. Activating the feature is straightforward: simply highlight the relevant section and press `Ctrl + K` on Windows or Command + K on Mac. This brings up a prompt where you can input instructions for the changes you'd like to see. The Inline Editor then generates updated code based on your input, which you can review, accept, or reject.

One practical example of real-time edits involves adding a dropdown menu to a navigation bar. Suppose your project already has a basic navigation bar with links to "Home," "About," and "Contact." To enhance functionality, you decide to add a dropdown menu under the "About" section with additional links to "Team," "Mission," and "Careers." Highlight the HTML or JSX code for the "About" link, activate the Inline Editor, and input a command like, "Add a dropdown menu with links to Team, Mission, and Careers under the About link." The AI responds by generating the necessary HTML and CSS (or JSX if you're working with React), ensuring the dropdown integrates seamlessly with the existing navigation bar.

Once the code is generated, it appears in a diff view, allowing you to preview the changes before applying them. This transparency ensures you're in control of the modifications and can make adjustments as needed. For instance, if the dropdown's design doesn't match your expectations, you can refine it further by providing additional instructions such as, "Style the dropdown menu with a white background, shadow effect, and hover animations."

Another example of real-time editing is changing the design theme of an application. Suppose your project currently uses a light theme, but you want to switch to a dark mode for a more modern look. Highlight the global CSS file or the root styles in your project, then activate the Inline Editor. Input a command like, "Switch the design theme to dark mode with a black background, white text, and muted accent colors." The AI updates the styles, adjusting elements like background colors, text colors, and hover states across the application. If you're using a CSS framework like Tailwind CSS, it may also add or adjust utility classes to achieve the desired effect.

Adjusting layouts is another frequent use case for real-time edits. For instance, suppose you're building a dashboard and want to change a card layout from a single-column stack to a grid layout. Highlight the section of code responsible for rendering the cards and prompt the AI with, "Convert the card layout to a responsive grid with three columns on desktop and one column on mobile." Cursor AI generates the updated code, incorporating responsive design principles and ensuring the layout adapts gracefully to different screen sizes.

The Inline Editor also excels at making small but impactful edits to text or content within the project. For example, you might want to update the placeholder text in a form field. Highlight the input element and ask the AI, "Change the placeholder text to 'Enter your email address.'" The AI makes the adjustment immediately, saving you time and effort compared to manually searching for and editing each instance.

Another advantage of the Inline Editor is its ability to handle cascading changes. For instance, if you decide to standardize the font size across your project, you can select a global CSS file or theme configuration and instruct the AI to "Set all paragraph text to 16px and all headers to a consistent scale." The AI makes the necessary adjustments and applies the changes uniformly, ensuring visual consistency throughout the application.

Cursor AI's Inline Editor isn't just about making changes; it's also a powerful tool for experimentation and iteration. If you're exploring multiple design options or testing different layouts, you can use the Inline Editor to quickly prototype variations without committing to them. For example, you could test a sidebar navigation layout against a top bar design by prompting the AI to generate both options and toggling between them to see which works best for your application.

The real-time nature of these edits ensures that you can see the results immediately. By combining the Inline Editor's precision with its responsiveness, Cursor AI empowers developers to iterate quickly and efficiently, turning ideas into polished features without the usual trial-and-error cycles. Whether you're adding functionality, refining aesthetics, or optimizing layouts, the Inline Editor provides a streamlined, intuitive way to enhance your projects in real time.

Integrating External Resources

Integrating external resources into a project is a critical aspect of development, especially when working on complex applications that require clear documentation, external dependencies, or tailored configurations. Cursor AI simplifies this process by allowing developers to add external resources like documentation, files, and links directly into their workflow, enabling more context-aware assistance and precise outputs. Additionally, the use of `.cursor_rules` files allows for project-specific behavior, giving developers greater control over how Cursor AI interacts with their code.

One of the key ways to integrate external resources in Cursor AI is by linking documentation. For instance, if you are working with a specific library or framework like Tailwind CSS, React, or a proprietary tool, you can provide Cursor AI with the official documentation link. This allows the AI to reference the material while generating or editing code, ensuring its suggestions align with the conventions and best practices outlined in the documentation. To add documentation, simply use the AI chat interface (`Ctrl + L` or `Command + L`) and input a command like, "Refer to the Tailwind CSS documentation here [link] and generate a responsive button component." The AI will access the linked resource and create code that adheres to the provided guidelines.

Beyond linking online documentation, Cursor AI also supports uploading files for enhanced context. Suppose your project includes a design specification document, a PDF manual, or a set of example code snippets. You can upload these files directly into Cursor AI, allowing it to analyze and reference them while assisting you. For example, if you upload a file containing design guidelines for your project, you can instruct the AI, "Follow the design standards outlined in this document to create a login form." This ensures that the generated code adheres to predefined specifications, reducing the need for manual adjustments later.

In addition to documentation and files, Cursor AI allows developers to integrate links to external resources such as APIs or data sources. For instance, if you're building an application that interacts with a REST API, you can provide the API documentation link and ask the AI to generate code for fetching and displaying data. A prompt like, "Use this API [link] to retrieve weather data and display it in a dashboard component" enables the AI to produce code that integrates seamlessly with the API, including authentication, data parsing, and error handling.

One of Cursor AI's most powerful features for customizing project behavior is the `.cursor_rules` file. This configuration file allows developers to define project-specific rules that the AI must follow. For example, if you are working on a Python project that adheres to strict PEP 8 formatting guidelines, you can include a rule in the `.cursor_rules` file specifying, "All Python code must comply with PEP 8 standards." Cursor AI will then ensure that any generated or modified code aligns with these rules.

Creating a `.cursor_rules` file is straightforward. Place a file named `.cursor_rules` in the root directory of your project and define the desired rules in plain text or JSON format. For instance, in a web development project, you might include the following rules:

json

Copy code

```json
{

  "language": "JavaScript",

  "framework": "React",

  "style": "TailwindCSS",

  "rules": {

    "components": "All components must be functional components.",

    "css": "Use Tailwind CSS for styling; avoid inline styles.",
```

```
      "testing": "Write tests for
all new components."

    }

}
```

These rules guide Cursor AI's behavior when generating or modifying code. For example, if you request a new React component, the AI will create it as a functional component styled with Tailwind CSS, and it may also suggest a test file to accompany it.

Another practical use of `.cursor_rules` files is for enforcing naming conventions or directory structures. For instance, if your team uses a specific folder hierarchy for organizing code, you can define this structure in the `.cursor_rules` file. A sample rule might look like:

json

Copy code

```json
{
  "structure": {
    "components": "src/components",
    "pages": "src/pages",
    "styles": "src/styles"
  }
}
```

With this rule in place, Cursor AI ensures that new components, pages, or styles are automatically created in the correct directories, reducing the risk of disorganization.

To enable or disable `.cursor_rules`, you can toggle the setting in Cursor AI's preferences. This flexibility allows you to decide when the rules should apply, making it easy to switch between projects with different requirements.

In practice, integrating external resources and using `.cursor_rules` files not only enhances the accuracy and relevance of Cursor AI's assistance but also ensures consistency across your project. Whether you're referencing documentation, uploading design files, or defining custom rules, these features empower you to tailor Cursor AI to your specific needs. This level of customization makes it an invaluable tool for maintaining efficiency and precision in modern development workflows.

Chapter 5: Tips for Maximizing Cursor AI

Best Practices for Beginners

When starting with Cursor AI, especially as a beginner, adopting best practices can significantly enhance your experience. Effective planning and clear communication with the AI are essential to achieving precise and valuable results. By structuring your tasks thoughtfully and crafting detailed prompts, you can harness Cursor AI's full potential and streamline your development workflow.

Planning Tasks for Accurate AI Responses

The foundation of successful interaction with Cursor AI lies in proper planning. Before diving into coding or making requests, take a moment to define what you aim to achieve. AI works best when given specific, discrete tasks rather than vague or overly complex instructions. Planning ensures you have a clear vision of your goals, which helps Cursor AI deliver relevant and effective outputs.

1. **Define Your Objective**

   Start by outlining the purpose of your project or task. Whether you're building a simple webpage, adding a new feature, or debugging code, clearly identify your objective. For example, instead of a general goal like "Create a webpage," specify, "Build a responsive landing page for a portfolio with a hero section, a contact form, and social media links."

2. **Break Down Tasks into Smaller Steps**

   AI performs better when given smaller, manageable tasks rather than broad, overarching requests. Breaking your project into steps allows Cursor AI to focus on one aspect at a time, reducing errors and ensuring consistency. For instance, if you're creating a landing page, divide the task into smaller parts such as generating the hero section, styling the contact form, and adding navigation links.

3. **Consider the Context**

Think about the context of your request and how it fits within the larger project. Ensure that the AI has access to the necessary information, such as project files, documentation, or design guidelines. Providing relevant context helps Cursor AI generate outputs that align with your project's style and structure.

4. **Prepare Any Required Resources**

If your project relies on external libraries, frameworks, or APIs, ensure they are installed and configured before starting. For example, if you're using Tailwind CSS, set it up in your project beforehand so that Cursor AI can incorporate it into the generated code seamlessly.

How to Provide Detailed Prompts for Better Outputs

Crafting detailed and specific prompts is key to effective communication with Cursor AI. The more precise and descriptive your instructions, the more accurate and useful the AI's responses will be.

1. **Be Specific and Clear**

   Use precise language to describe what you want. Avoid ambiguous terms or overly broad instructions. For example, instead of saying, "Make a form," provide details like, "Create a login form with fields for email and password, styled with Tailwind CSS, and include a submit button."

2. **Specify Frameworks and Tools**

   If your project uses specific frameworks, libraries, or tools, include this information in your prompt. For instance, "Generate a React component styled with Tailwind CSS" provides the AI with the necessary context to produce relevant code.

3. **Include Functional Requirements**

   Describe the functionality you need in detail. For example, if you're adding a dropdown menu, specify its behavior: "Add a dropdown menu under the navigation bar's 'Services' link. The menu should appear on hover and include links to 'Web Development,' 'App Development,' and 'SEO Services.'"

4. **Describe Visual or Design Preferences**

   If you have specific design preferences, mention them in your prompt. For example, "Style the button with a gradient background from blue to green, rounded corners, and a hover effect that changes the text color to white."

5. **Reference Existing Code or Files**

   If your request involves modifying or building upon existing code, highlight the relevant section or file. For example, "In the `Navbar.js` file, add a sticky navbar feature and update the styling to match the site's dark mode."

6. **Ask for Explanations or Suggestions**

   If you're unsure about how to proceed, you can ask Cursor AI for recommendations. For example, "What's the best way to implement authentication in a React app using Firebase?" This not only provides you with guidance but also helps you learn and improve your coding skills.

7. **Iterate and Refine**

   After receiving an output, review it carefully. If it's not exactly what you need, provide additional instructions to refine the result. For instance, "The login form looks good, but please add a 'Remember Me' checkbox and align the submit button to the center."

Examples of Effective Prompts

- "Create a responsive header for a webpage with a logo on the left and navigation links on the right. Use Tailwind CSS for styling."

- "Write a function in JavaScript that validates an email input and returns true if it's valid and false otherwise."
- "Update the `Footer.js` component to include the current year dynamically and style it with a light gray background."
- "Explain the purpose of the `useEffect` hook in React with an example."
- "Add a modal popup that appears when a button is clicked. The modal should have a close button to hide it."

By combining thoughtful planning with detailed prompts, you can unlock Cursor AI's full potential. These practices ensure that the AI understands your requirements, minimizes errors, and provides outputs that align with your expectations. For beginners, this approach not only simplifies coding but also builds confidence in navigating AI-assisted development.

Workflow Optimization

To maximize the potential of Cursor AI, it's essential to understand when and how to use its key features—**Composer**, **Inline Editor**, and **Chat Window**—effectively. Each tool serves a specific purpose and, when used strategically, they can streamline your workflow, reduce redundancy, and enhance productivity. Combining these features in a cohesive way ensures seamless coding and efficient project management.

When to Use Composer

The Composer is Cursor AI's most powerful tool for handling large-scale or multi-file operations. It is ideal for situations where you need to generate significant portions of a project or make structural changes across multiple components.

1. **Starting a New Project**
   When creating a new project, use the Composer to generate foundational files and

components. For instance, if you're building a web application, you can instruct the Composer to create a folder structure, boilerplate code, and essential files like `index.html`, `styles.css`, and `app.js`.

Example Prompt:

- ○ *"Set up a React project with components for Header, Footer, and MainContent. Style the application using Tailwind CSS."*

2. **Creating Multiple Components**

Use the Composer when you need to generate multiple interconnected files or components. For example, when adding features to a website, such as a contact page, a services page, and a portfolio section, the Composer ensures consistency across all files.

Example Prompt:

- ○ *"Generate a portfolio webpage with a grid layout for images, a sidebar for*

*navigation, and a footer with social
media links."*

3. **Making Batch Changes**

   If you need to apply a specific feature or
   functionality to multiple files, the Composer
   is your go-to tool. For example, adding a
   footer component to all pages or updating
   the theme across the project can be handled
   efficiently.

   Example Prompt:

   ○ *"Add a dark mode toggle button to all
   pages in this project, ensuring the
   styles adapt accordingly."*

The Composer excels in handling complexity and
large-scale operations. However, it's less suitable
for smaller, targeted tasks or quick iterations,
where the Inline Editor and Chat Window come
into play.

When to Use Inline Editor

The Inline Editor is perfect for making precise, context-aware changes to specific sections of code. It allows you to refine existing components, update styles, or fix bugs without leaving the editor.

1. **Editing Specific Sections**
   When you want to tweak a particular element, such as changing the color of a button or updating the text in a header, the Inline Editor is the most efficient tool.
   Example Prompt:
   - *"Change the button color to a gradient from blue to green and make the text bold."*

2. **Adding Functionality to Existing Code**
   If you're building upon existing components, such as adding hover effects to a navigation menu or integrating a modal, the Inline Editor provides quick and accurate updates.
   Example Prompt:

- *"Add a dropdown menu to the 'Services' link in the navbar with links to 'Web Development,' 'SEO,' and 'Content Writing.' The menu should appear on hover."*

3. **Debugging or Fixing Errors**

When you encounter errors or need to revise a specific section of code, the Inline Editor is invaluable. Highlight the problematic section, activate the editor, and input a prompt like, *"Fix this function to handle edge cases for null inputs."*

4. **Refining Styles and Layouts**

Use the Inline Editor to adjust CSS properties or fine-tune layouts. For instance, aligning a div to the center or making a section responsive can be handled seamlessly.

Example Prompt:

- *"Make this section responsive, ensuring it displays in a single column on mobile devices."*

The Inline Editor is your tool of choice for rapid, precise edits, but for broader context or questions, the Chat Window offers additional versatility.

When to Use Chat Window

The Chat Window is best suited for exploratory tasks, seeking advice, or interacting with the AI to better understand code. It excels in providing explanations, generating small snippets, and answering questions.

1. **Generating Code Snippets**

   If you need a standalone function or component, the Chat Window can generate it quickly. For example, generating a utility function for calculating discounts or a simple login form.

   Example Prompt:
   - *"Write a JavaScript function that calculates the factorial of a number."*

2. **Explaining Code**

   Use the Chat Window to understand

unfamiliar or complex code. You can paste a block of code and ask the AI for a detailed explanation.

Example Prompt:

- ○ *"Explain what this function does and identify any potential issues."*

3. **Asking General Questions**

If you're unsure about a framework, library, or best practices, the Chat Window serves as a reliable assistant.

Example Prompt:

- ○ *"What's the best way to implement authentication in a React application using Firebase?"*

4. **Searching Through Codebase**

When working on larger projects, the Chat Window can help you locate specific variables, functions, or files.

Example Prompt:

- ○ *"Where is the* `calculateTotal` *function defined in this project?"*

5. **Integrating External Documentation**

   If you're using a new library or API, link its documentation and instruct the Chat Window to generate code accordingly.

   Example Prompt:

   - *"Use this API documentation to create a weather dashboard that displays temperature and humidity for a given city."*

Combining Features for Seamless Coding

To optimize your workflow, consider how these features complement each other and use them in tandem for a streamlined experience.

1. **Start with Composer for Large Tasks**

   Begin by using the Composer to generate the project's structure and foundational components. For instance, set up a React app with a header, footer, and main content area.

2. **Refine Components with Inline Editor**

   Once the structure is in place, use the Inline

Editor to fine-tune individual components. Update styles, add interactivity, or adjust layouts with targeted edits.

3. **Leverage Chat Window for Guidance and Assistance**

   Throughout the process, rely on the Chat Window to answer questions, explain code, or provide recommendations. Use it to generate utility functions, explore best practices, or integrate external resources.

4. **Iterate and Improve Continuously**

   Combine the features for iterative development. For example, after using the Composer to generate a form, refine its design with the Inline Editor and seek validation logic from the Chat Window.

By strategically integrating the Composer, Inline Editor, and Chat Window into your workflow, you can enhance productivity, minimize redundant tasks, and focus on creativity and problem-solving.

Cursor AI becomes not just a tool but a collaborative partner in your development process.

Troubleshooting Common Issues

While Cursor AI is a powerful tool for streamlining the development process, like any technology, it can occasionally generate content that needs refinement or clarification. Understanding how to troubleshoot common issues with AI-generated content ensures you can maintain productivity and achieve accurate results. This section covers two major areas: debugging AI-generated content and handling irrelevant or overcomplicated suggestions.

Debugging AI-Generated Content

AI-generated code, while highly useful, may sometimes require debugging to ensure it functions as intended. This is especially true for complex tasks or when working with incomplete or ambiguous prompts. Here are practical steps to debug and improve the code generated by Cursor AI:

1. **Understand the Generated Code**

   Before implementing AI-generated code, review it thoroughly. Use Cursor AI's **Chat Window** (`Ctrl + L` or `Command + L`) to ask for an explanation if a section of the code isn't immediately clear. For example:

   - *"Explain how this function works and identify any potential issues."*

2. By understanding the code's purpose and logic, you can identify potential problems early.

3. **Test the Code Incrementally**

   Integrate AI-generated snippets into your project one piece at a time. Testing smaller sections helps isolate issues and ensures new additions don't disrupt existing functionality. For example, if Cursor AI generates a new API integration function, test its output with sample data before integrating it into the main application.

4. **Check for Missing Dependencies**

   Cursor AI may occasionally overlook certain

dependencies or setup steps, especially for tools, libraries, or frameworks. If the generated code references an undefined variable, library, or module, ensure the required dependencies are installed. Use Cursor AI to generate missing configurations or consult official documentation for setup instructions.

- ○ Example Prompt: *"Fix the missing dependency in this React component and ensure it renders correctly."*

5. **Use Debugging Tools**

Leverage built-in tools like browser developer consoles or debugging libraries to trace errors. For instance, if the AI generates JavaScript code that throws an error, use `console.log()` statements to trace the issue or inspect the network requests in your browser's developer tools.

6. **Validate Against Standards**

AI-generated content might sometimes deviate from best practices or coding standards. Use linters and formatters (e.g., ESLint for JavaScript) to identify inconsistencies. If standards aren't followed, you can refine the code manually or instruct Cursor AI:

- *"Rewrite this code to comply with PEP 8 standards for Python."*

7. **Modify and Re-Prompt**

If an issue persists, highlight the problematic section of code and use the **Inline Editor** (`Ctrl + K` or `Command + K`) to refine it. Provide specific instructions, such as:

- *"Optimize this function to handle edge cases where the input is null or undefined."*

By iteratively testing and refining, you can ensure the AI-generated content aligns with your project's requirements.

Handling Irrelevant or Overcomplicated Suggestions

At times, Cursor AI might generate suggestions that are irrelevant, overly complex, or misaligned with the intended task. Addressing these scenarios effectively involves clear communication and strategic adjustments.

1. **Provide Clear and Detailed Prompts**

   Irrelevant outputs often stem from ambiguous or insufficiently detailed prompts. To avoid this, specify your requirements precisely. For example, instead of saying, *"Create a function to process data,"* use:

   - *"Create a function in JavaScript that takes an array of numbers, filters out negative values, and returns the sum of the positive values."*

2. **Simplify Overly Complex Outputs**

   If Cursor AI generates code that seems unnecessarily complicated, simplify the problem for the AI. For instance, if a generated solution uses advanced features or obscure libraries, rephrase your prompt to request a more straightforward approach.

- Example: *"Simplify this algorithm to achieve the same result without recursion."*

3. **Adjust AI Behavior with Context**

Use `.cursor_rules` files or context-specific instructions to guide the AI's behavior. For example, if you prefer concise code, include a rule: *"Avoid verbose implementations and use standard libraries where possible."* Cursor AI will then adapt its outputs to your preferences.

4. **Iterate on Suggestions**

If the initial output isn't relevant, refine your prompt to clarify the goal or exclude unnecessary elements. For example:

- First Prompt: *"Generate a React component for displaying user profiles."*

- Refined Prompt: *"Generate a functional React component to display user profiles. Include props for username, avatar URL, and bio, but avoid using external libraries."*

5. **Leverage Feedback Mechanisms**

Cursor AI allows for feedback loops where you can critique the generated code and provide further instructions. Highlight a specific section and ask the AI to revise it, for example:

- *"This function is too complex. Simplify it while maintaining performance."*

6. **Review with a Critical Eye**

AI-generated content isn't infallible, and it's essential to approach outputs critically. Look for common pitfalls, such as:

- Redundant code.
- Over-reliance on less familiar libraries.
- Logical errors or edge cases not handled.

7. When you spot these issues, address them directly with specific instructions or refine the code manually.

8. **Practice Incremental Changes**

   If the AI suggests a series of changes or a complex feature, implement them incrementally. Break the task into smaller parts and prompt Cursor AI for each step, ensuring each piece is accurate before moving forward.

Example Scenario: Debugging and Refining

Scenario: Cursor AI generates a JavaScript function for sorting an array, but it's overly verbose and includes unnecessary custom logic.

- **Initial Output**:

  javascript

  Copy code

```javascript
function sortArray(arr) {

    if (!Array.isArray(arr)) {
```

```
        throw new Error("Input
must be an array");

    }

    for (let i = 0; i <
arr.length; i++) {

        for (let j = i + 1; j <
arr.length; j++) {

            if (arr[i] > arr[j])
{

                let temp =
arr[i];

                arr[i] = arr[j];

                arr[j] = temp;

            }
```

```
        }

    }

    return arr;

}
```

- **Refined Prompt**:

  "Simplify this function to use JavaScript's built-in sort *method instead of nested loops."*

- **Updated Output**:
  javascript
  Copy code

```
function sortArray(arr) {

    if (!Array.isArray(arr)) {

        throw new Error("Input must be an array");
```

```
        }

        return arr.sort((a, b) => a -
    b);

    }
```

By refining the prompt, the revised code is simpler, more efficient, and aligns with best practices.

Troubleshooting common issues with Cursor AI is a skill that improves with practice. By combining thoughtful prompts, iterative refinement, and critical evaluation, you can overcome challenges like debugging errors and handling irrelevant suggestions. These strategies ensure you get the most out of Cursor AI, empowering you to build robust, high-quality code with confidence.

Chapter 6: Challenges and Limitations

Understanding AI's Boundaries

While Cursor AI is an exceptional tool for enhancing coding efficiency, it's important to recognize its limitations. AI is a powerful assistant, but it is not a substitute for human judgment and expertise. Knowing when to step in manually and how to balance AI-generated content with your own insights is critical for successful development.

Scenarios Where Manual Intervention is Necessary

1. **Complex Business Logic**

   AI struggles with intricate domain-specific logic that requires deep contextual understanding or adherence to unique business rules. For example, an AI may generate a generic algorithm for calculating taxes but might overlook regional regulations or exceptions. In such cases, human expertise is essential to tailor the solution.

2. **Debugging and Error Handling**

   While Cursor AI can identify and fix simple errors, debugging complex issues often requires a deeper understanding of the project. For instance, runtime errors related to data inconsistencies or integration points with external systems may require manual investigation and resolution.

3. **Custom Design Requirements**

   AI-generated design elements might not perfectly match specific aesthetic or branding guidelines. For example, while Cursor AI can create a responsive navbar, achieving a pixel-perfect design aligned with a company's style guide often requires manual adjustments.

4. **Security and Performance Optimization**

   AI may not always account for best practices in security and performance optimization.

For example, an AI-generated authentication flow might work functionally but lack measures such as input sanitization, encryption, or rate limiting. Reviewing and enhancing these aspects manually is crucial to ensure robust and secure code.

5. **Handling Ambiguity**

   Cursor AI performs best with clear instructions, but ambiguous or vague requirements can result in generic or irrelevant outputs. For example, asking for "a form for user input" without specifying fields or validation criteria may yield a basic form that doesn't meet your needs. In such cases, refining your prompt or manually modifying the code is necessary.

Balancing AI Assistance with Human Expertise

1. **Set Realistic Expectations**

   Understand that AI is a tool, not a solution. Use it to handle repetitive tasks, generate boilerplate code, or provide suggestions, but rely on your expertise for critical decision-making and problem-solving.

2. **Combine AI with Manual Adjustments**
Treat AI-generated code as a foundation. Review, test, and refine it to meet the project's unique requirements. For example, if the AI generates a function for API integration, test it thoroughly to ensure it handles edge cases and errors appropriately.

3. **Leverage AI for Exploration, Not Final Outputs**
Use Cursor AI to explore ideas, learn best practices, or generate drafts. For instance, if you're implementing a new library, ask the AI for an example setup and then adapt it to your project.

4. **Maintain Control of Project Direction**
Avoid relying on AI to define the scope or structure of your project. While AI can assist with execution, the overall vision and design

should be driven by your expertise and understanding of the project goals.

Navigating Common Pitfalls

Adopting Cursor AI, especially for beginners, can come with a learning curve. Understanding common pitfalls and applying strategies to refine AI interactions ensures a smoother and more productive experience.

Overcoming the Learning Curve for Beginners

1. **Start Small**

   Begin with simple tasks to build confidence. For example, use Cursor AI to generate a basic HTML page or a JavaScript function. Gradually work on more complex features as you become familiar with its capabilities.

2. **Learn by Asking Questions**

   Use the AI Chat Window to ask for explanations and learn coding concepts. For instance, if the AI generates a function using useEffect in React, ask it to explain the hook and its use cases. This approach helps bridge knowledge gaps and enhances your coding skills.

3. **Experiment with Prompts**

Beginners may initially struggle with crafting effective prompts. Experiment with different ways of phrasing instructions to discover what works best. For example, compare these two prompts:

   o *"Create a form."* (Too vague)
   o *"Generate an HTML form with fields for name, email, and password. Include validation for required fields."* (Clear and specific)

4. **Take Time to Understand Outputs**

Resist the temptation to accept AI-generated code without understanding it. Review the code, ask questions, and test it to ensure it aligns with your expectations and functions correctly.

5. **Use External Resources**

Supplement your learning by referencing official documentation, tutorials, or guides. For instance, if the AI generates a snippet using Tailwind CSS, review Tailwind's official documentation to understand how the utility classes work.

Tips for Refining AI Interactions Over Time

1. **Craft Clear and Detailed Prompts**

The quality of AI-generated outputs heavily depends on the clarity of your instructions. Always include relevant details such as frameworks, expected functionality, or design preferences. For example:

- Instead of: *"Create a webpage,"* say: *"Generate a responsive webpage with a navbar, hero section, and footer. Use Tailwind CSS for styling."*

2. **Iterate and Provide Feedback**

Treat AI interactions as a collaborative

process. If the output isn't ideal, refine your prompt and try again. For example:

- Initial Prompt: *"Generate a login form."*
- Refinement: *"Generate a login form with email and password fields, a submit button, and error messages for invalid input."*

3. **Utilize Project-Specific Rules**

Use .cursor_rules files to guide AI behavior in your projects. For instance, if your team uses a specific naming convention, include rules like: *"All component files should follow PascalCase naming (e.g., UserProfile.js)."*

4. **Review Outputs Critically**

Always review AI-generated content for logical errors, inefficiencies, or deviations from best practices. Don't assume the output is flawless; approach it as a starting point that may require refinement.

5. **Leverage Feedback Loops**

Cursor AI allows you to revise and improve

generated content through feedback. Highlight a section and input detailed instructions for revision. For example:

- ○ *"This code works, but it's too verbose. Simplify it by using array methods like map or filter."*

6. **Track Your Progress**

   Over time, you'll notice patterns in the AI's responses and become adept at crafting effective prompts. Keep notes of successful prompts and workflows to build a personal playbook for interacting with Cursor AI efficiently.

Understanding AI's boundaries and navigating its common pitfalls are essential skills for maximizing Cursor AI's potential. By recognizing when manual intervention is necessary and balancing AI assistance with your expertise, you can achieve higher-quality results. For beginners, taking the time to overcome the learning curve and refine interactions ensures a smoother and more productive experience. With thoughtful planning and continuous learning, Cursor AI becomes a reliable partner in your coding journey.

Chapter 7: The Future of Coding with Cursor AI

Artificial intelligence has fundamentally reshaped the coding landscape, transforming how developers approach problem-solving, collaborate, and execute projects. AI tools like Cursor AI are at the forefront of this revolution, blending the precision of traditional programming with the efficiency and adaptability of machine learning. By automating repetitive tasks, offering real-time suggestions, and enabling faster iterations, AI-driven development has become a cornerstone of modern software engineering.

AI's Role in Development

AI's impact on development extends far beyond convenience—it redefines what developers can achieve within limited timeframes. Traditional coding often involves extensive trial-and-error cycles, debugging, and manual configuration. AI eliminates many of these bottlenecks by analyzing patterns, suggesting optimal solutions, and adapting to the context of a project in real time. For instance, Cursor AI not only generates code snippets but also contextualizes them within a larger application, ensuring they align with the project's architecture and design principles.

One of the most significant ways AI reshapes development is by democratizing access to coding. Beginners, who may find traditional programming intimidating, can now leverage AI to overcome initial hurdles. Cursor AI, for example, simplifies the process of setting up projects, writing boilerplate code, and debugging errors. A beginner who previously struggled with creating a responsive webpage can now achieve this within minutes using AI-powered tools. This lowers the entry barrier and accelerates learning curves, empowering more individuals to enter the tech industry.

Experienced developers also benefit from AI's capabilities, particularly in areas that demand speed and scalability. Tasks that previously required hours of manual effort, such as configuring complex backend systems or integrating APIs, can now be completed in a fraction of the time. AI allows developers to focus on higher-level decision-making and creative problem-solving rather than repetitive and mundane tasks. For instance, Cursor AI's inline editing feature lets developers refine existing code instantly, enabling rapid iteration and enhancing productivity.

Another transformative aspect of AI is its ability to facilitate collaboration. In a team setting, AI can act as a mediator, ensuring consistency across codebases, enforcing style guides, and even suggesting improvements during code reviews. Cursor AI's potential in this area is immense, as it can automate much of the grunt work involved in collaborative projects, such as merging changes, resolving conflicts, and documenting updates.

Looking ahead, AI's role in development is poised to expand even further. The integration of machine learning models into coding environments, as seen with Cursor AI, is just the beginning. Future innovations will likely include tools that can predict project outcomes, optimize workflows based on historical data, and even recommend strategies for achieving business goals through software. For example, Cursor AI could evolve into a platform that not only assists with coding but also provides insights into project timelines, resource allocation, and market trends, enabling developers to make informed decisions at every stage of the development lifecycle.

As AI becomes more integrated into development, ethical considerations will also play a crucial role. Developers and AI platforms alike must ensure that AI-generated code is secure, efficient, and free from biases. Cursor AI, with its emphasis on transparency and user control, sets a strong precedent in this regard. Its privacy modes and configurable settings allow developers to tailor its behavior, ensuring alignment with project requirements and ethical standards.

Expanding Cursor AI's Capabilities

Cursor AI is already a powerful tool, but its true potential lies in its ability to evolve and adapt. Emerging features and experimental tools are set to expand its capabilities, making it an even more indispensable asset for developers. These advancements promise to revolutionize how Cursor AI interacts with users, integrates with other technologies, and enhances development workflows.

One of the most exciting innovations in Cursor AI is the introduction of AI reviews. This feature leverages machine learning to analyze codebases, identify inefficiencies, and suggest improvements. Imagine a scenario where a developer submits a pull request, and Cursor AI not only reviews the code for syntax errors but also highlights potential performance bottlenecks and security vulnerabilities. This level of automated code review ensures higher-quality outputs and reduces the burden on human reviewers, allowing them to focus on strategic decisions rather than nitpicking minor details.

Long-context chats are another groundbreaking feature under development. Traditional AI tools often struggle with maintaining context in large projects, leading to fragmented and inconsistent outputs. Cursor AI's long-context chats aim to address this limitation by enabling the AI to retain a deeper understanding of the project's structure, objectives, and history. For instance, a developer working on a multi-module application can ask Cursor AI about a specific function written weeks earlier, and the AI will reference it accurately within the broader context of the codebase. This capability significantly enhances productivity and reduces the cognitive load on developers, as they no longer need to repeatedly provide context for their queries.

Experimental tools, such as Cursor AI's ability to generate code from visual inputs, are also on the horizon. These tools aim to bridge the gap between design and development, enabling developers to upload Figma files or other design assets and receive corresponding HTML and CSS code. While this feature is still evolving, its potential is immense. For instance, design teams can create mockups that developers can instantly transform into functional prototypes, streamlining collaboration and accelerating product timelines.

Another area of expansion is the integration of Cursor AI with other development technologies. Modern software engineering relies on a diverse ecosystem of tools, frameworks, and platforms. Cursor AI's ability to interface with these technologies will determine its long-term relevance and utility. For example, integrating Cursor AI with version control systems like Git can automate tasks such as commit message generation, branch merging, and conflict resolution. Similarly, compatibility with popular CI/CD pipelines could enable Cursor AI to assist with testing, deployment, and monitoring, further embedding it into the development lifecycle.

Cursor AI's integration with cloud services like AWS, Azure, and Google Cloud also opens up new possibilities. Developers could use Cursor AI to configure and manage cloud infrastructure, deploy scalable applications, and even optimize costs by analyzing resource utilization. For instance, a prompt like, "Set up a serverless backend on AWS for this application," could result in Cursor AI provisioning the necessary resources, writing deployment scripts, and providing documentation—all within minutes.

As these capabilities expand, Cursor AI must also address challenges related to scalability and user customization. The introduction of features like `.cursor_rules` files demonstrates a commitment to personalization, allowing users to define project-specific guidelines that the AI must follow.

Future iterations could take this further by enabling team-level configurations, where project leads can set overarching rules for their teams, ensuring consistency and alignment across collaborative efforts.

In conclusion, Cursor AI is not just a tool but a continuously evolving platform that reflects the dynamic nature of software development. Its role in reshaping the coding landscape is already evident, and its potential for future innovations promises to make it an even more integral part of the developer's toolkit. By introducing features like AI reviews, long-context chats, and experimental tools, and by integrating seamlessly with other technologies, Cursor AI is set to redefine how software is conceived, developed, and deployed. For developers, this evolution represents an opportunity to work smarter, create faster, and achieve greater impact with every project.

Conclusion

Cursor AI has redefined how developers approach coding by offering a blend of efficiency, accessibility, and innovation. This guide has walked you through every aspect of this powerful tool, from its installation and initial setup to advanced functionalities like real-time editing, project creation, and troubleshooting. Along the way, you've learned how Cursor AI streamlines workflows, simplifies complex tasks, and empowers developers at all skill levels to achieve more in less time.

At its core, Cursor AI is a tool designed to adapt to the unique needs of its users. Beginners can leverage it to break through initial challenges, gaining confidence as they experiment with generating code, understanding new concepts, and building projects from scratch. Experienced developers can use it to automate repetitive tasks, enhance code quality, and scale their efforts by focusing on more strategic aspects of development.

Features like the Inline Editor, Composer, and Chat Window work together seamlessly, creating a dynamic and intuitive environment where productivity flourishes.

The guide has highlighted how Cursor AI supports a wide range of workflows, from creating entire projects to refining small code segments with precision. Its ability to integrate external resources, handle project-specific rules, and offer real-time suggestions ensures that it remains relevant across diverse coding scenarios. Moreover, Cursor AI's forward-looking features—such as long-context chats, AI reviews, and experimental tools—showcase its commitment to evolving alongside the needs of modern developers.

The journey doesn't stop here. While this guide provides a solid foundation for understanding and using Cursor AI, the true value of the tool lies in exploration. Every prompt, feature, and interaction offers an opportunity to uncover new possibilities. Whether it's experimenting with design-to-code workflows, integrating custom models, or tackling complex collaborative projects, Cursor AI invites you to push the boundaries of what's possible in software development.

To fully harness the potential of Cursor AI, it's important to keep learning and experimenting. Resources like official documentation, online coding communities, and advanced courses on AI-driven development can further enhance your skills. Exploring open-source projects that utilize Cursor AI can provide real-world insights and inspire innovative solutions. By engaging with these resources and consistently applying the techniques shared in this guide, you can build a strong foundation for mastering Cursor AI and achieving greater success in your coding endeavors.

This guide aims to equip you with the knowledge and confidence to integrate Cursor AI into your workflow and embrace its transformative potential. As you continue your journey, remember that Cursor AI is not just a tool—it's a partner in creativity and problem-solving. By combining its capabilities with your expertise and imagination, you have the power to shape the future of development and unlock new levels of productivity and innovation. The path ahead is full of opportunities, and Cursor AI is here to help you make the most of them.

www.ingramcontent.com/pod-product-compliance
Lightning Source LLC
Chambersburg PA
CBHW071007050326
40689CB00014B/3522